John Jacobson's RISER CHOREOGRAPHY

A Director's Guide For Enhancing Choral Performances

Demonstration Choir: New London Singers, New London, WI
Lori Flury, Director

7777 W. BLUEMOUND RD. P.O. BOX 13819 MILWAUKEE, WI 53213

Contents

INTRODUCTION

Centuries ago in a small Italian town (I'm absolutely making this up) nine-year-old Anthony Wenger (of Italian-German-Norwegian ancestry), joined the Grand Cathedral Choir! He loved so much the rehearsals, the choir robes, the altos. Every Thursday night he would join the throngs of choristers in the chapel for two hours of rehearsal and every Sunday morning he sang his heart out in the Choir's "hymn of the week." They would line up in four slightly curved rows on the floor in front of the altar, women and girls in the front, men and boys in the back. It was glorious indeed!

The only problem with the entire situation was that nine-year-old Anthony (Tony to his friends) was short. Really short! And all of the girls and women were tall. Really tall! Every Sunday when the choir would process to their assigned positions, poor Tony was lost in a forest of belt buckles and bustles, with only the vaguest idea of where the congregation was, to say nothing about the conductor. As exciting as the music was for Tony, the whole scenario was regularly frustrating as he couldn't see a thing. His grandmother in the thirteenth pew was equally distressed at not being able to see her little "angel" virtually buried in the fourth row of the GCC (Grand Cathedral Choir).

So, early one Sunday morning as the choir was just about to enter the sanctuary, in a brazen act of ingenuity and desperation, Tony made a suggestion that would change the course of choral music for all time! "Say!" he tried to sound casual, "Why don't we all back up a couple of feet so that the back rows can stand on the steps leading up to the altar? That way we can all see and be seen!" He knew the moment he said it that he was totally out of line.

There were gasps and guffaws from the rest of the choir! One soprano actually swooned! The choir director offered her resignation and the organist pulled out all the stops! "Blasphemy!" "Scandalous!" Even cries of "Stone him!" were heard! Tony knew that his days in the GCC were numbered. His insides trembled. And then. . .

"I think that Anthony has a good idea!" It was the countertenor Guido Petrucci, who was also very short. He had been staring into the back of Anna Maria Graziano's rapidly graying hair for thirty years and had finally realized that there may actually be better things to stare into the back of.

"Guido!" "Guido!" "Guido!" was all anybody could even think of saying as they shook their heads, except for the few who muttered "Tony! "Tony!" "Tony!" beating their breasts and pulling on their hair in impassioned attempts at self flagellation.

But, thanks to Guido's seniority, when the time came for the choir to sing, the timid conductor gave a nod of hesitant approval and the choir took their places at the front of the congregation. Except this time, for the first time, the sopranos stayed on the floor, the altos stood on the first step, the tenors took the second and the basses towered above the rest on the top. Choral risers were born!

For the ensuing centuries that is the way it has remained. One choir, four rows, three steps. Oh sure, someone came along and decided that it would be nice if the choir could bring the steps of the cathedral "on the road" with them when they visited other congregations full of sinners, and since they were pretty heavy marble, they put them on wheels. Later someone even figured out how to make collapsible steps that were easier to transport in an ox cart. (I believe that this actually occurred in a small town in Ohio in 1957 when school transportation budgets were cut for co-curricular activities other than athletic events.) Someone else added a fourth and, on occasion even fifth step to the structure for greater height. Never-the-less, things remained pretty much the same for quite a few hundred years. Every concert would begin with the choir processing onto the risers in single file as the audience watched in utter astonishment. The bigger the choir, the longer the line, the more the astonishment. If your choir was so big that it took fifteen or twenty minutes to file onto the stage, you were considered quite the master conductor and actually could get by with performing a lot less music to fill up an evening's concert. The longer the entrance took, the greater the conductor's job security.

And then. . .(I'm making this up again.)

In a Lutheran church (ALC of course) somewhere in Wisconsin, amidst a concert of heady music and fervent testimony, a young boy of questionable background and ancestry looked up at his mother from the pew they shared and asked a little too loudly, "Why in the world don't they DO something?!"

He was quickly shuffled off to a ultra-liberal university and was forced to wear a sequined star on his jacket emblazoned with the words "ONLY DOES SHOW CHOIR."

By now you are probably asking yourself "What in the world is this book about?" Fair enough question.

This book is for choral directors of any level of experience and with any kind of choir who:

- Have found themselves in situations where they have a huge choir with very little space. The "chandelier-in-the-soprano-section" syndrome.

- Realize that we live in a world where our audiences are used to a lot of visual stimulus and are lost with old-fashioned, static performances that still work great for radio and recording situations, but seem inadequate for many of your "live" situations.

- Would like to add a little movement to your choir's performances but don't want to leave the risers and don't want to move into the world of full blown dance.

- Have looked at that big block of singers and wondered if there weren't some other ways they could be positioned to be more interesting to look at without hurting the sound we've worked so hard to perfect.

- Realize that singing is a total physical activity and have wondered if your choir might actually sing more musically with even a very small amount of movement included in their rehearsals and/or performances.

- Have done a lot of choreography with your choir but find yourself creatively stifled when trying to stage your ballads and more traditional selections, or with large numbers of performers.

- Have a principal who looks up from his/her concert seat and innocently asks the question, "Why don't they DO something?"

YOU MUST ALWAYS STAGE

Like it or not, if you are the director of a "live" musical performance, one in which you invite an audience to listen and watch your choir, you ARE a staging director and you MUST make staging choices as well as musical ones. For instance, if you choose to have your choir parade onto the stage in long, single file rows you are saying to your guests (the audience) that you have decided that this is the very best and most effective way of presenting your choir. You are saying that, "of all the choices available to me, this is the mood and look that I want as our first impression." Your CHOICE is legitimate! On occasion, long, single file rows WILL be the very best way to begin your concert! But, you need to understand that you had choices and this is the one you felt was the most effective. You CHOSE it.

Now, doesn't it feel good to realize that your first choice as a staging director has already been made? You've recognized that your guests deserve attention to ALL of the elements of your concert; detailed attention, like that which you give to your music. Once you have made it over this first hurdle, all of the rest will seem easy and perhaps on occasion, exhilarating!

If you have your choir stand in four, even rows with one shoulder slightly turned toward the director for the first selection in your performance, that was a staging choice, too. And, it might be a very effective one. It might be good for your second and third number as well! However, if by your fourth, fifth and sixth selection you are still standing in that staid position, you probably need to reconsider the attention span of a modern audience. You might experiment with the many options that are available to you, many of which are easy to implement and dramatic in their result.

This book is about some of those choices that are available to you when designing your concert performances. It is about **how to use risers**. It is not rocket science. Thank goodness! But, it *will* introduce you to ideas that have worked for others in your situation and may even spark new and creative ideas that are in you just waiting to be expressed. We have divided the book into anticipated questions that choir directors might pose. Starting from the most simple thought to some intricate and subtle changes in your choir's formations.

Where Do I Begin?

Let's take it from where we're "AT."

FILING ON

Notice how much nicer it appears to the audience if, when your choir is walking on, you send the front row first as opposed to the back row. In this way, the natural adjusting and shuffling that needs to happen is somewhat camouflaged by an already-in-place front row.

Front row stationary while back rows file on

It is sometimes a safe idea to have the top row walk first to the next-to-the-top level and then step up all at once.

Top row walks to second step, then all step up to third step

If you have the luxury of being able to enter from both sides of the stage you can obviously get your choir in place twice as fast by sending one row from each side. Try sending rows one and three from one side and two and four from the other.

First and third rows enter from right, second and fourth rows enter from left

Try having two rows enter from each side at the same time to cut down your entrance time by a huge amount.

If you have the luxury of having extra choral risers try setting them up as steps going off the back of the top riser. See how dramatic an entrance can be made by having all or some of your choir enter en masse up and over from behind.

Entering from behind the risers

With this same arrangement you could enter a row or two from each side, plus one or two up and over the back for a rapid and dramatic entrance.

Front two rows entering from sides, back two rows enter from behind

If you have the facility, try having your rows enter from all over the auditorium at once. Through the audience, from the wings, up and over the back of the risers are all effective entrances.

Entering from all over the auditorium

THE SCRAMBLE

This is a way of mounting the risers that says to your choir, "You've got this much time to get there, now get there." This should be used for a very quick entrance that will surprise your audience and let them know that they are in for something different and unpredictable. The choir members could come from anywhere in the auditorium, or from off stage, including perhaps even from audience chairs.

The scramble

You may even try the SCRAMBLE type entrance using music from the first song of your performance. This would work for a slow song that needs to build or the introduction or first verse of an up-tempo song. It would even be effective to enter from all over the place singing a traditional madrigal processional selection.

O.K. You're There, Now What?

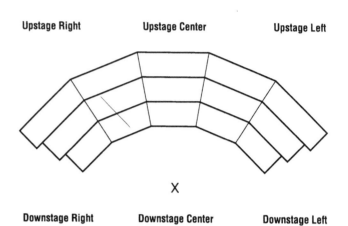

Upstage Right   Upstage Center   Upstage Left

X

Downstage Right   Downstage Center   Downstage Left

Stage areas

BLOCK FORMATION

The most traditional choice is to have the entire block choir focus their eyes on the director so that he/she can truly lead them through the musical selection. The cleanest way to have your choir stand is with their outside foot slightly forward and pointing at the director. Those on stage right will have their right foot forward. Those on stage left will have their left foot forward. This gives a very unifying "line" to each individual's body and to the group as a whole. This is called a "closed" position.

Choir in closed position

Choir in open position

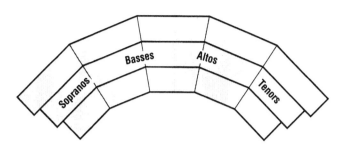

Soprano, basses, altos, tenors

There are lots of ways to line up in the BLOCK formation.

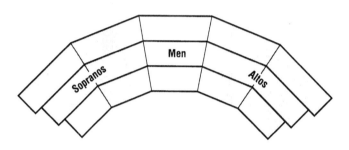

Sopranos left, Men in the middle, Altos right

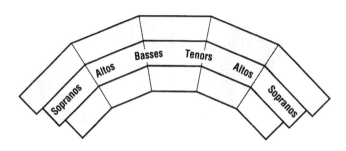

Sopranos, altos, basses, tenors, altos, sopranos

Sometimes these changes in formation will help the sound in selections that call for a different mix.

Out Of A Few, Many

If three rows are good, six are great! See how easy it would be to have every other person in each row step either forward or back so that you suddenly have twice as many rows. This will not hurt your vocal sound at all, but will be a nice visual change for the audience, and will even make your choir feel as though they suddenly have their "own" space.

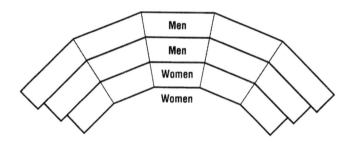

Men in the back rows, women in the front

Choir in three rows

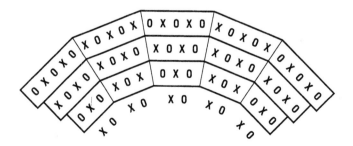

Mixed block formation

Choir in six rows

Try performing your first two or three numbers in three rows and then make the move to six for a couple of numbers; or two rows to four, four to eight, or five to ten!

Standing In The Windows

This means that the second line of people is standing back and in-between the members of the row in front of them. That "space" between the two people in front is called the "window."

The window

Choir standing in the windows

Body Angle Changes

Now, see what happens when the choir simply changes the angle of their body to the audience. Try having the entire cast simply turn their bodies slightly one direction or the other. The change is very subtle, but refreshing to the audience.

Choir facing stage left

Another choice is to have the entire cast suddenly turn so that their shoulders are square to the audience. This straight-on posture is a sudden change but will have a fresh look, good for a song or two.

Choir with shoulders square to the audience

Now have the cast turn away from center so that the two halves of the stage are actually back to back with each other.

Choir turned away from center

Focus Changes

O.K. director! Let's really go out on a limb. Move yourself from the center of the stage. Unless you're going to sell advertising space, it's not the most exciting view for the audience anyway! See what happens when your choir is able to change their focus from downstage center to stage left or right. They can still look at you. You can still lead them. But, the audience is getting a new look.

Director moves to stage right

If you're really brave, remove yourself entirely for a number and have the choir perform "on their own" or with the accompanist. See what they can do with subtle changes in visual focus.

For instance:

• Have them sing a lullaby and pretend to be looking into a cradle downstage center.

Choir looking at "cradle" during lullaby

• Allow your cast to look from stage left to stage right as they sing an appropriate phrase like, "O beautiful for spacious skies, for amber waves of grain. . ."

• Have them look in a big arch from left to right to sing of "rainbows," "visions," "dreams" or "blue skies."

• Have them lift their eyes from low to high for phrases like "For purple mountain majesties. . ." or "To dream the impossible dream. . ."

• Notice how the choir can control where the audience's focus will be. If the entire choir is looking at one person, say a soloist, so will the audience look at that person.

Choir focuses on soloist

Sometimes your point of focus needs to be very calculated, to the point of being mechanical. For instance, see how powerful it can be to have the entire cast focus their eyes on one specific place, over the heads of the audience, at the back of the auditorium. Pick a spot like an "EXIT" sign or the lighting booth. This will give the impression of inspiration and vision even as your choir is concentrating on pitch, tone quality and, hopefully, the emotional message of their music.

Choir focusing over audience's heads

Notice how effective even a dispersed visual focus can be. With the entire cast choosing their own focal point the audience is given the impression of many individuals each singing their own song, lost in their own thoughts.

Choir with many different focal points

You will eventually see that these changes in focus and body angle are effective from any of the many formations available to you beyond the basic BLOCK formation that we have discussed so far.

OTHER FORMATIONS

There are unlimited positions that your choir can assume other than a simple BLOCK formation, and beyond the multiple row approach. Here are a few of the most accessible ones that will serve as a starting place and, possibly a catalyst for more creative line-ups.

Bowling Pin

A basic Bowling Pin formation is a line up of singers with one person in the front row, two in the second, three in the third, and so on, like the line up of bowling pins at the end of the alley. This pyramiding effect can go on to include as many people as you have in the choir or until you run out of room on the stage.

Bowling pin

There are many ways to vary the Bowling Pin formation to give it a different appearance to the audience. Each of the alternatives sends a different emotional message to the audience and can help direct or re-direct their focus.

Reversed Bowling Pin

This simply means that the longer rows are downstage and the "point" of the pyramid is the furthest upstage.

Reversed bowling pin

Angled Bowling Pin

This would have the "point" of the formation somewhere that puts the pyramid at an oblique angle to the audience. Again, notice the variety of "looks" you can create by changing the performer's body angles and/or focus.

Angled bowling pins

Imagine if that point person was a soloist, or even just your best visual performer. You will be surprised at how that person in the front will make the audience visualize a group that is all as effective as that one.

Open and Closed Bowling Pins

An "open" formation just means that you have allowed space between each of the performers. This gives the formation a more spread-out look. A "closed" formation would have each of the performers side by side and close to the row in front of them. This is a more compact look.

Open bowling pin

Closed bowling pin

Notice what interesting pictures you can make on stage with more than one Bowling Pin formation at once. Try two side by side.

Side by side reversed bowling pins

Try two regular and a reversed in the middle.

Two regular and one reversed bowling pins

Reverse that formation, and have two reversed with a regular in the middle.

Two reversed and one regular bowling pins

See how the three Bowling Pin Formations together give you a block formation. But with different costumes or genders in each of the pyramids you have an interesting, even artistic, look.

Christmas Tree

A fun opportunity to use a Bowling Pin Formation is to reverse it so that the point is far upstage and on the top riser. Give everybody in the formation a flashlight covered with red or green cellophane and you'll have yourself a fairly convincing "living Christmas Tree." For variety, you could have the outline of the tree have one color flashlight and the inside have another. Have the point of the tree even hold a star if you're really ambitious.

"Living" Christmas tree

Diagonal Lines

There are an unlimited amount of options for stage design using lines of performers at different angles. Try, for instance, two or three lines going up each side of the risers with each of the singers slightly off the shoulder of the singer in front of them. The choir is all facing directly downstage giving them a stair-stepping look. This will leave a space in the middle of the riser.

Diagonal lines square to the audience

See how this picture changes when everyone turns slightly to face downstage center as opposed to directly downstage.

Diagonal lines facing downstage center

What if all of the diagonal lines are on one side of the riser facing stage center or straight at the audience for two more effective looks.

Facing stage center

Facing straight at the audience

Put a line or two of singers across the top riser and one or two more perpendicular to that going directly down mid stage from that top line to the base of the risers. Now you have the makings of a "cross" formation on stage.

Cross formation

With enough people and a big enough stage you could do three crosses side by side, or rearrange your diagonal lines to make a star, a diamond, a square or a triangle.

Three crosses

Half circle with focus directly downstage

Triangle

Half Circles

Half circles are easy to move into from a BLOCK formation or from any other for that matter.

Try a single file half circle. This will take up a lot of room, but with a small enough group, it might work for you. This is especially good for a group that is working without a conductor because they can easily make eye contact with one another and work more effectively as a group.

Like we did with the BLOCK formation, have every other person in your single half circle step forward or back and we will have double or even triple half circles. The move itself is interesting staging as the audience watches your cast seemingly grow before their eyes.

Double half circle

Again, you can experiment with changes in focus and body angles.

Shoulder to shoulder half circle

Double half circle with focus downstage

See the change that happens in that half circle when the body angle and focus is moved from downstage center to directly downstage.

Convex Half Circles

This would suggest that the "ends" of the half circle(s) are far upstage with the center of the half circle closest to the audience. This may not initially seem like the most useful formation when facing directly at the audience, although it can work in the right setting. However, look at what an interesting way to present a small group or soloist if the half circle turns to face upstage center to the highlighted performers.

Convex half circle

Turned to featured soloist

Full Circles

It is an easy staging adjustment to take two half circles and make them into one. Risers can help you elevate the back of that circle so that everyone can still be seen.

Full circle

Sometimes the action of going from one position to the next is fascinating for the audience. There are several ways to go into a full circle from halves. If the front of two concave half circles simply walks forward to make a convex half circle, you have one full circle. This is one of the best ways your choir can highlight a song with a message of "brotherhood" or "unity" without singing or saying a word.

Another interesting way to move from "halves" to "whole" is to begin with two or three concave half circles and then have two of them follow in single file one left and one right to meet in the front. The remaining row (if there were three) can become the back of the circle and the other two, the sides and front.

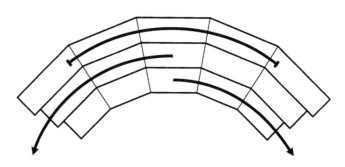

Forming a full circle

Double and Triple Circles

From one big circle, every other person steps into the center and you have double circles. One forward and one back and you have triples, one inside the next.

Double full circles

For an interesting look have the circles walk around their own circumference, either all in one direction or each circle a different direction.

Family Portrait

There is no formula for the family portrait position other than everybody being situated so they can all see and be seen. This is like a family having their picture taken. Some are kneeling, sitting, standing, squatting. Some could be seated on stools or ladders, on the edge of the stage or on another person's knee so that there are a great variety of levels being used.

The big difference will be seen in the degree of "friendliness" in your portrait. The more "closed" your formation, the more friendly the picture. Notice how body contact, even between a single couple can make a pose go from being cold to friendly.

Closed family portrait

Open family portrait

Unfriendly couple

Friendly couple

Nature's Risers

Even before Anthony Wenger's discovery of the riser as we now know it, we were all blessed with the best "elevators" of all in the form of our knees. Many different levels can be achieved with no mechanics at all simply by bending your knees. These gifts should be used extensively, especially in more casual Family Portrait poses to give natural dimension to your staging choices.

NOVELTY FORMATIONS

There are many ways to place your choir on stage to suggest a picture appropriate to the song you are performing. These will be fun to have in your "bag of tricks" for just the right song at the right time.

Ship/Boat Motifs

If the entire choir faces one direction and puts their upstage foot on a riser, then uses their hands as if they were operating oars, you will present the suggestion of a boat full of rowers. This may be all the staging you need for songs like "Way Down Upon the Swanee River," Paddlin' Maddlin' Home," or "Sentimental Journey."

Boat full of rowers

Using one line of performers all facing the same direction with the end people standing up straight and those toward the middle of the line getting progressively lower, you have a wonderful long boat, reminiscent of George Washington crossing the Delaware.

Long boat

Two long lines perpendicular to the audience and bowed in the middle will present a semblance of a huge Viking ship. You can even have a mast head down front with one person between the two arching rows.

Viking ship

If some choir members sit on the floor like they are in a toboggan, bending their knees, and rowing with both hands, you will create a row boat on stage. Together with a couple of the other boat motifs and you have a stage full of sailors.

Row boat

Bus

Four rows of singers with an aisle in between, will give the suggestion of a school or city bus. Put a driver on a stool at the front of the line for real authenticity. When will you need a bus motif? How about for songs like "The People On The Bus Go Up And Down," "On The Road Again," or "We Go Together"?

People on a bus

Cars

Put two people in the front seat, two in the back and two or three more sitting backwards way behind (if you have a station wagon) and your choir looks like they are in the middle of an interstate highway.

Riding in a car

Train

The entire cast facing one direction and churning their arms with bent elbows gives the look of a locomotive. You could rearrange them in rows and blocks of people to resemble passengers in a coach, dining car or even sleeper. Great for songs like "Chattanooga Choo Choo," "Sentimental Journey," or "California Here I Come!"

Riding in a train

Subway

All facing one direction, hold a brief case in your downstage hand and the balance strap in your other and you'll look like a choir full of commuters on the "'A' Train," "The Rattle Of A Subway Train. . .", or "New York, New York, A Heck Of A Town. . ."

Riding in a subway

If you liked the cars, boats, busses and subways, wait until you put your choir in a sleigh ride!

Sleigh Ride

Have all of the choir sit or kneel on the risers in a tight box formation. This can be done straight toward the audience or at an angle downstage one direction or the other. If you connect the rows with one hand to the shoulder of the person sitting in front of you, you will have something that looks very similar to an old-fashioned sleigh ride, or a wagon, or a coach, or even a "Surrey With A Fringe On Top!"

On a sleigh ride

Add a few "horses" down front for a comical ride "Over The River And Through The Woods", or "reindeer" for "Here Comes Santa Claus" or "Jingle Bells."

Sleigh ride with horses

Cracking the whip

Ocean View

Use a BLOCK formation with every other row swaying in the opposite direction and your chorus begins to look like a body of water. From here you can do the wave, add a swimmer or even a shark for just the right song like "Under The Sea" or any song about surfing.

At the ocean

Carriage Ride

Put two or four people sitting side by side in rows of two and you can create the look of a carriage ride. No other choreography might be necessary to get your point across for songs like "Don't Fence Me In," or "Sweet Betsy From Pike."

Carriage ride

So What Kind Of Risers Are We Talking About?

Choral risers have come along way since A. W.'s creative use of the Cathedral steps so long ago. There are entire corporations that specialize in the design and marketing of the many varieties of modern day risers. They have become increasingly portable, compact, collapsible, varying in width, design and height. They are made of wood, aluminum, steel or alloy.

There are long, skinny risers, short, fat risers, triangular risers, square boxes, orchestral platforms, risers that have expandable stairs, risers with railings, risers with removable legs that can be substituted with varying heights, carpeted risers, light-weight risers and risers that "weigh a ton!" Let's look at a few of the many possibilities that are available to you and different ways that you can use the ones that have been collecting dust in the janitor's storage room since your last concert.

THREE, FOUR, OR FIVE STEP CHORAL RISERS

These are basically stair cases. Usually they have steps of anywhere from twelve to twenty-four inches in depth. Note that it is a lot easier to stand and move on sixteen, twenty or twenty-four inches than it is on twelve. You will also notice in regards to cost and portability, there is little difference between a twelve and twenty-four inch step. If you are purchasing a new set of risers, it is strongly suggested that you opt for the wider steps as they will give you much more flexibility when it comes to making your staging choices.

The heights of these risers are fairly standard. The bottom step is usually about eight inches high; the second, sixteen; the third, twenty-four; the fourth, thirty-six. On occasion, you will come across risers that begin at twelve inches and go up in twelve inch increments as opposed to eight. If you are designing and constructing your own risers, or purchasing new ones, you might seriously consider going with the higher steps as this will offer a more dramatic presentation on the stage.

Many times risers such as these will have an optional

extension at the top, so that a standard three-step riser can convert to four, or a four-step riser to five. With the higher risers, one should also consider a waist high guard railing across the top, and maybe even down the sides for obvious safety reasons.

Standard choral risers

ORCHESTRAL PLATFORMS (BAND RISERS)

These risers were originally designed to be used by concert bands or orchestras with enough room for everyone to have a chair and a cello between their knees. However, they work great for choirs, too!

Most of these platforms come in a standard four foot by eight foot width and length. Although you will occasionally come across slight variations on this standard. Of course, if you make your own platforms you can design them for your own needs and make them any size you wish. Like the choral risers, these band risers come in gradually increasing heights from as low as four to six inches to as high as thirty-six and even forty-eight inches. They usually have either collapsible or even removable legs for easier storage and height options. In the business, they are often referred to as "hernia platforms" because they are the ones that generally weigh about the same as the combined weight of the baritone section! Many a fine choral director has slipped a disk or popped a vessel hauling out the band risers for the annual "Spring Sing!" The trick with these platforms is to DELEGATE! Gratefully, some of the riser companies have begun to develop much lighter weight materials to build these platforms that are just as sturdy as the old cast iron type.

The wonderful thing about these platforms is their versatility and their stability. They can hold a lot of singers and withstand a lot of motion. You can create almost the same choral formations on these platforms that you can on the so-called "choral risers." You can make Block formations, Half Circles, Whole Circles, Bowling Pins,

Diagonal Lines, Diamonds, Crosses, and all of the other novelty arrangements we have already discussed. What's great is that you can also go much further with these risers simply because of the space that a four by eight platform allows you. With this width, you can move onto more involved choreography while still maintaining the height variations that help your audience see everyone on stage.

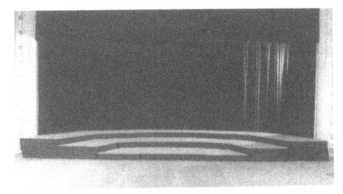
Standard orchestral platforms

You can also rearrange these platforms to make a lot of interesting stage designs on top of which you build your show. Here is an example that is fairly basic:

Photo Courtesy of Wenger Corporation

COMBINING ORCHESTRAL PLATFORMS AND CHORAL RISERS

If you work with a piano, combo or a full band you can even put them in the middle of your choir for a unique look, excellent sound, and a unified performing ensemble. If you are lucky enough to own both orchestral platforms and choral risers, or if you can at least talk the band/orchestra director out of his/hers for a time, you have at your fingertips the opportunity to create a lot of different arrangements on stage.

First of all, you can stack choral risers on top of the orchestral platforms to really build a lot of height. Just make certain that they are securely fastened together so that the choral risers don't slip from the top of the orchestral platforms. You can also use your choral risers as stair steps on and off the orchestral platforms. Try having your choral risers set up in reverse, backed up to the top platform for rear exits and a safety net for the highest risers. Again, make certain that the higher you build, the more safety features you build into your construction. This should include braces, railings, wiring risers together and glow tape to clearly mark the edges

BOXES AND TRIANGLES

There are commercially available triangular boxes and square platforms that take a more modular approach to riser structure. They usually come with collapsible sides that serve as legs when held in place by a triangular or square lid. This lid becomes the top and the part the performer stands on. These "pods" can be put together in a variety of ways to make many different set designs. One thing that you want to keep in mind is to make certain that the actual space on top of these risers is big enough that it offers room to perform. If a triangular shape is only big enough to adequately hold one person dancing or two standing perfectly still, you may want to opt for a larger size or a different shape. It is difficult to dance on the points of a triangle. However, when two of those triangles are put together the square space that they make can be an excellent dance area. One of the tricks then becomes, holding those two triangles together so that your square doesn't suddenly split apart and your singers disappear into the abyss! One very "low-tech" way of doing this is to take industrial strength duct tape and literally tape your stage together. Now you are probably thinking, "If I'm going to tape two triangles together to make a square performing space why not just start off with a square platform?" Good point. Do it.

What this "pod" or "modular" approach to risers does for you is it allows you the flexibility to change your set design in the middle of your show. Of course, you could try to do this with risers of any size, but these smaller units are designed specifically for such maneuvers. Make sure that you rehearse these on-stage changes many times so that they are quick, fluid and not a burden to the viewer.

See what kind of creative "Family Portraits" you can come up with by actually splitting up the platforms and spreading them out in various positions and combinations on the stage.

Photo courtesy of Wenger Corporation

Now That We've Made Our Formations, What Kind Of Moves Can We Do That Won't Hurt Our Singers Or Each Other?

So glad that you asked!

Let's make one very bold statement right off the bat.

"You can't cover up bad singing with all of the wonderful staging, choreography, costumes, lights and glitz in the world. If the music is bad, fix it first. Then, once you've accomplished that, you can move into all of the other elements that will help you amplify that already effective artistic endeavor. The music is the core."

Now, let's talk about the rest!

In truth, you will sometimes find that adding a little, or even a lot of movement to your singing will actually help your cast to sing MORE musically. Singing IS a total physical activity that takes total physical involvement, from the top of your head to the bottom of your toes. What better way to demonstrate that physical nature of music than to move your body to it?

It is indeed selfish for a choral conductor who stands waving his/her arms and moving his/her body to the music to then expect his/her singers to stand rock-still and make beautiful and expressive music. With very young singers, it is also true that they like to wiggle when they sing. In fact, they like to wiggle even when they don't sing. You have the opportunity to focus that wiggling into expressive choreography. That's it! Controlled wiggling! The key to successful song and dance!

The good news is that, as a choral director, you don't have to get involved in full-blown dance moves to add effective movement to your choir's performance. You don't have to take yourself out of the performance, go sit down and get out of the way. You don't have to rent Radio City Music Hall to have room for your performers to execute their show. You don't even have to have your choir leave the comfort and security of the risers that they have grown to know and love! There is a lot that you can do "where you are at!"

CHORALOGRAPHY

Choralography is a term that is used to describe movement that enhances vocal music but does not want or warrant being called "dance." Many would suggest that choralography is mostly movement from "the waist up" that can often be performed with a minimum of space. The best choralography is that which helps the singers better express the lyric or the musical line of the selection they are singing. Here's a good "for instance" that most will recognize.

We have all participated in performances of the "Hallelujah Chorus" from Handel's "Messiah." We have all been frustrated by a chorus of singers who insist on making the "jah!" of the word "Hallelujah!" the syllable of accent. It's very easy to do. In a rehearsal situation, try having your singers raise their right hand high above their head on the first syllable of the word and gradually bring it back down to their side as they finish the word. In other words, the hand shoots into the air on the "Hal" and is back to your side by "jah!" With this type of action, which so obviously places the emphasis on the first syllable and de-emphasizes the final, you will be amazed how quickly the vocal line which is being reflected in your arm movement becomes habit. Now, if you decide that doing "choralography" to the "Hallelujah Chorus" in real performance situations is not your cup of tea, you can eventually leave out the arm movement. You will find however, that singing the piece with the accent on the first rather than the last syllable has become ingrained in your choir's memory. Movement has helped make your choir MORE musically accurate!

The "Hallelujah Chorus"

Being an outrageous liberal I would suggest that there is no music that has ever been written that cannot be appropriately choreographed, even the "Hallelujah Chorus"! After all, didn't the king himself rise to his feet on its first hearing? Song and dance has been a legitimate art form since the cavemen first discovered their version of Rock 'n' Roll! Even in the Bible there are so many references to singing, dancing, shaking your timbrels and other paraphernalia! (Especially in the John Jacobson Revised Standard Version.) There's no universal right or wrong in our dynamic art, just a whole world of potential and possibility. How wonderful that one art form can actually enhance and embellish another!

Another example of how movement can actually help you sing more musically is to take a phrase of any song that has a musical crescendo toward the middle and a decrescendo toward the end. For instance, Kirby Shaw's "Jubilate Deo." By the end of the first "Jubilate Deo" there is a peak point in the crescendo. The second "Jubilate Deo" has a gradual decrescendo. To have your choir physically act out the musical line allow them to scoop one arm from low to high on the line that crescendos and slowly lower that same arm as the decrescendo occurs. They are now doing with their arm what you want them to imitate with the volume and intensity of their voice. It will help them visualize what you want them to do with the musical line. They will understand that the music has a contour and linear movement to it just as the arm gesture reflects. Again, you may choose to limit this move to a rehearsal situation or actually incorporate it into a performance setting. You will be amazed at how much an audience "hears" with their eyes. If they "see" the contour of the musical line they very often will hear and understand it similarly.

"Jubilate Deo"

THE DALCROZE EURYTHMIC APPROACH TO LEARNING MUSIC AND MUSICALITY

This method utilizes a great deal of movement including arm gestures, clapping, walking, running and stretching through space like the music itself. It is a very effective way to teach and understand music, its lines, rhythms, and contour. Using these techniques in rehearsal or performance is legitimate as long as it is enhancing the process of making the music more effective or heightening the performance experience.

CHOREOGRAPHING THE WORDS

There are two obvious choices for designing choreography or choralography for a choir, be they riser-bound or not. One is to examine the music itself and see how physical movement could enhance the musical goals and character of the piece. In this case you are literally "dancing to the music" and letting it dictate the message of your moves.

The second approach is consideration of the lyrics of your musical selection. Examining the poetry of the song and figuring out how a physical movement could enhance the message is probably the most common approach to staging. Of course, some of the best choreography will no doubt reflect both the lyrics *and* the musical character of the song.

There are simple gestures that are almost universal in their understandability. They are very often the best moves to utilize in your staging because they will help your listening viewers and your performers appreciate the song's message most accurately. Almost any logical move will work if the move is executed with total commitment. Singing the phrase "Two little eyes to look to God," while holding up two fingers pointing to your eyes and praying as you look up to God, may seem amazingly juvenile and even trite. However, if a small child or choir of children is singing the song and executing the gestures with total heart and commitment, it is, in truth, the perfect choreography!

"I like you and you like me!" sung while pointing first to yourself, then to your audience, and then back to yourself, seems embarrassingly simplistic. However, when a performer on stage performs those moves to the lyrics with full passion and honest commitment these "simplistic" moves are the perfect enhancers.

What Are Some Other Universally Recognized Gestures And Postures That Can Help To Artfully Express The Lyrics Of A Song Even If The Choir Is Limited In Space And Movement Experience?

FISTS

Fists can show strength, power, "rock!" (as in rock 'n' roll), anger, determination, intensity, might, vigor, force, authority, ability, "Yes!," "yeah!," "Rah!," "Go!" Fists can be used at your sides, on your hips, punched into the air, punched across your front at chest level, or while marching.

Fists punched in air

Fists across front at chest level

Fists while marching

Fists at sides

Fists on hips

HANDS CLASPED TOGETHER

This motion can be used to show praying, praise, reverence, angel, please?, wishing, hoping, begging, appeal, togetherness, brotherhood, "one," trust, power, bondage, patriotism. You can use hands clasped together in fists, with fingers intertwined, with fingers straight, at chest level or overhead.

Hands clasped together

OUTSTRETCHED ARM WITH PALM UP

Use this motion to show taking, receiving, "come," I need, I want, hold, lift, carry, receive, get.

Outstretched arm with palm up

OUTSTRETCHED ARM WITH PALM DOWN

This will show there, go, give, send forth, you, take (as in "take this from me."

Outstretched arm with palm down

BOTH ARMS OUTSTRETCHED

Many times, this will mean the same as the above two gestures depending on whether the palm is up or down and whether or not the movement of the arm is toward or away from the body. If the outstretched arms are held out in front of you with your palms up, but lower than your shoulders you present a message of questioning or presentation, as if to say "take me" or "take this." If you modify this arm gesture ever so slightly, it can present a silent question, "why?" "where?" or others.

Both arms outstretched

TRAVELING GESTURES

Train Arms

While making fists, bend at your elbows to ninety degrees and churn the arms like the wheels of an antique locomotive. This move is easily understood and appropriate for a lyric, or an entire song about trains, journeying, traveling, steam boats, moving along, on the road, etc.

Train arms

Traveling Arms

This motion is like the gesture that a basketball referee uses to indicate a traveling violation in a game. This churning of the arms is great for a lyric about movement, roll (as in "rock 'n' roll"), songs with a Latin beat, and others. The move can be executed directly in front of the performer, off to one side, high or low, or with variations happening simultaneously with in the group. This step is very simple, but very effective for many instances.

Traveling arms

Hitch-hiking

Putting your thumb out like a road side traveler is a clear indicator to your audience that the message of this lyric has to do with travel, going along down the road, moving, etc.

Hitch-hiking

The Search

This move is taken from the real life action of shielding your eyes from the sun as you look for something in the distance. Dancers of the 1960s and 70s made this simple move into an actual routine. It sends a clear message of looking for someone, something, or someplace. It also can indicate "far off," "over there," or "where?" For example, "Where, oh where has my little dog gone?" or "Little old lady from Pasadena!"

The search

Walking Or Running Knee Pops

Legs together with the knees bending alternately will give the dancer a look of movement without actually going anyplace. This is useful for lyrics about walking, strolling, "getting along," running, moving. For example, "Walking my baby back home. . ."

Knee pops

HANDS BEHIND YOUR BACK

Hold your hands high in the small of your back and you will look as though you are at ease, but alert and ready to go. Sometimes this will be referred to as "stand by" position, as though the performer is standing in readiness to do something else, like sing or dance.

Stand by position

With your hands behind back held lower so that there is little or no space between your elbow and your sides, you will send a message of shyness or pouting.

Hands behind back held lower

SALUTES

There is no move more recognizable than a salute to indicate a military or patriotic message. There are several variations of a traditional military salute that might be used depending on the occasion, the seriousness of the material or even the song's good humor.

Military Salute

Palm down, finger tips just above the eye brow, elbow angling to the side.

Military salute

"Gomer Pyle" Salute

A cartoon-inspired salute that turns the palm out at the forehead.

"Gomer Pyle" salute

Chest Level Salute

Another formal salute that raises the hand to the chest level. Without actually saluting this move gives the look and feel of pride that a regular salute suggests.

Chest level salute

Four-Count Salute

This uses the action of the salute to become a piece of choreography.

(1) Raise hand to forehead and bend knees.

(2) Raise hand high overhead and straighten legs.

(3) Lower hand to your side. (4) Rest.

HELD HANDS IN ROWS

A blatant show of brotherhood, friendship, love, unity, this is also an excellent way to get your spacing more exact. When your choir first lines up on the risers or off, have them hold hands. This activity will allow them to feel their way to even spaces on both sides of them.

Held hands in rows

BELL ARMS

Performed in one tempo, held hands moving forward and back like the clanging of a bell will give a message of joy and even childishness. Performed slower and with a greater deliberation, you might send a message of friendship and brotherhood.

Try lifting the arms a quarter of the way up and then down. Then raise them half way up and then down; three-quarters and down; all the way up and down.

Bell arms

HELD HANDS OVERHEAD

By standing still or swaying ala "We Are The World," you have a natural look of unity and brotherhood and it is easy to encourage audiences to join in both the singing and the movement.

Held hands overhead

MICKEY MOUSE EARS

Use jazz hands on top of your head. Not the most useful, but universally recognized!

Mickey Mouse ears

POINTING UP

This can mean up, high, higher, sky; but will also be appropriate for lyrics that have to do with God, heaven, liberty, one.

Pointing up

JAZZ HANDS

A "jazz hand" is simply a wide open hand with fingers spread and palm toward the audience.

Jazz hands

JAZZ HANDS OVERHEAD

This can suggest the sun, a star, a light, brightness, etc., especially if you shimmy it while you hold it overhead.

Jazz hands overhead

How Can You Use Simple And Obvious Gestures Without Making Them "Trite"?

Sometimes there are uncomplicated stylizations that you can add to a move that will make even the most literal, and perhaps even simplistic, gestures appropriate pieces of choreography. For instance, look at what happens to the moves for me and you if, instead of simply pointing to yourself and then your audience, you use both hands placed on your chest and then reach those hands to the audience.

Reach to yourself

Reach to the audience

Notice how a point at your audience is more of a dance if the choir members simple turn their bodies so that they are facing one side of the stage and the point is executed with the downstage hand.

Point facing one direction

For an even stronger move, one could add a lunge toward the audience on the point or the reach.

Point with a lunge toward audience

Consider a move for the word "hear" or "listening." A hand to the ear is obvious, but not very showy. Try lunging slightly the direction that you are "listening."

Lunge toward direction you are "listening"

See how the move becomes more of a dance even if the hand is slightly away from the ear as opposed right next to it. This demonstrates the idea that your moves most often should simply resemble the gesture you would use in regular conversation. The creative part of being a choreographer is designing new variations of ways to present words and gestures we use all the time and that are universally recognized.

"Listening" with hand away from ear

Seeing or Eyes

PRESENT ARMS

This gesture uses one or both arms to "present" your audience as though they were a prize in a game show. With your palm up, and your right arm stretched out to the left in front of your chest, move it from left to right.

Present arms

Try the same move with your left hand beginning from your right and moving to the left.

Say or sing the word "you" or any lyric that suggests "all of the people" and instead of pointing at the audience, "present" your arm from one side of the stage to the other. This move gives the same message as pointing your finger at your audience, but is more beautiful to look at, more inclusive and more polite!

SEEING OR EYES

Sweep one or both hands in front of your eyes when you sing a lyric about seeing, eyes, vision, etc. For example, "I Can See Clearly Now."

TILTING HEADS

Notice how a simple tilt of your head from left to right, or better yet and entire chorus of tilting heads, gives the look of simplicity and/or happiness. For example: "Tis A Gift To Be Simple."

CLAPPING

Clapping on stage is as much, if not more, a visual effect as it is an aural one. The clapping generally needs to look like it's making a sound. It does not have to be loud unless you are particularly using the sound of the clap for a desired effect.

STAGE CLAP

A "stage clap" usually means clapping the fingers of one hand into the palm of the other. This will give you a higher pitched, lighter sound that will cut through the din of other sounds on stage without overpowering the music. It can "look" loud without actually being so. If you need a lower or more "thudding" sound to your clap you could use more of the hand.

It is a fascinating exercise to experiment with different clap patterns being performed sequentially or simultaneously by different performers on the stage. The resulting sounds can be very exciting. For instance, try having the entire cast begin by clapping on beats two and four of a measure. Repeat this for several measures eventually allowing part of the group to double-time their claps so that they are clapping on every beat of the measure. Then, allow another section of the choir double time those claps so that they are clapping eighth notes against the quarter notes of the second group and the half notes of the first. You never even have to leave the risers to create some stage excitement with innovative clapping patterns!

SNAPPING

The snapping of your fingers, like clapping, can add effective human percussion to riser choreography. You can create patterns of sound incorporating clapping, snapping, slapping your thighs, beating your chest, or anything else that makes a musical and rhythmic sound.

SWAYING

Swaying, although simple, is sometimes the most difficult move to get uniform. A good way to begin is to think of leading with your shoulder. In other words, the shoulder is the first part of your body to go the direction that you are swaying. Practice it in an exaggerated style until everyone is looking basically the same. Then, tone down the movement for a more subtle effect.

Swaying

A nice picture can be created by having all of the cast assume a variety of poses, like a family portrait some kneeling, standing with one foot up a step, etc, and swaying.

A family portrait swaying

SWAY SNAPPING

In many respects sway snapping is easier to do than a simple sway. A sway snap allows the performers to "step touch" with both hands swinging the same direction as the sway and snapping their fingers on the "touch." This step is easy because every part of your body is moving in the same direction. The swinging hands and stepping feet help to keep it uniform and together. O.K. you'll probably have one beginning performer going just the opposite of everyone else, but just put two big people on either side of them and they will eventually get into the "swing" of it.

Sway snapping

NODDING

While limited to riser movement, it's amazing how effective a simple nod can be when used to enhance an accent or a line. Nod on beats one and three while changing your focus from stage left to right for a song like "Here We Come A-Caroling." Nod once on the down beat of each measure for a song like "Joshua Fit The Battle Of Jericho." Each voice part nod on the down beat of sequential measures.

FOCUS

The focus of each individual performer's eyes, and the entire cast's eyes, is one of the most important staging decisions that a director needs to make. No choice you make will be more visually profound than this. There are many choices. Maybe you have decided to have all of the eyes on the conductor wherever he/she might stand. You have probably realized by now that downstage center is not the only available choice.

Focus downstage center

See how powerful a visual effect is when the entire cast looks at a single place at the back of the auditorium, above the heads of the audience (say an exit sign or the lighting booth). This can be a very inspirational pose.

Focus at the back of the auditorium

Try having your performers drop their chins down to look at the floor and then slowly raise them up to look again at the exit sign. This is a very simple but profound move. Try it at different tempos and with appropriate lyrics. For instance, use a slow four counts and sing "For Purple Mountains Majesties." A little faster look works great for "Another Opening, Another Show" as we watch the curtain rise.

Try having everyone in the cast choose their own focus point "somewhere out there." This gives the audience the feel that there are a lot of individual performers on stage, each with their own story to tell.

Many different focal points

With the entire cast looking, at a uniform tempo, from left to right or right to left can be very useful. It helps the audience get the message of a cast looking out at the entire world, across "the amber waves of grain," or just singing about humanity.

Notice how focus can be used to help the audience know where they should be looking at any given moment. Focus can set off a soloist if all of the rest of the cast has their eyes on that soloist. It can also be used to keep attention away from a certain area if there is a set being moved or a bit of staging being set up for a later effect.

Focus on soloist

OPERA HANDS

This refers to clasped fingers at breast bone level like an old-fashioned and very formal opera singer in recital. This will usually come off quite comical to a modern day audience.

Opera hands

Clap

FLEXED HANDS

Bend your wrists with flat hands. This is usually quite feminine in appearance and especially good for moves reflective of the 1920s.

Burst

Flexed hands

CLAP BURST

Clap and follow it with a burst of your hands like fireworks.

BURST CLAP

Stretch jazz hands up and then clap.

Both the CLAP BURST and BURST CLAPS can be performed at varying degrees depending on the amount of space available. They are good examples of how visually effective clapping can be.

But How Can We Perform Real Live Dances Without Ever Leaving The Risers And Maybe Not Even Moving Our Feet?

PERIOD/STYLE DANCES

There are a lot of ways that performers who are confined to risers or very small dance areas can do movements that reflect actual dances but do not compromise the space or the sound. This is especially true for period dance styles where the dances have already been designed for you and all that you have to do is modify them to the requirements of your show. For instance, learn an entire dance of any period, say the 1920s dance called the Charleston. Now, try performing all of the routine again using only the moves that occur from the waist up. You will probably have a lot of "jazz hands" moving back and forth at about shoulder level. You might have some slapping of the thighs like you do in a full "chug" dance step. You may have some clasped fists moving left and right like the arm movements used in a "Shorty George." You could have some "scissoring" jazz hands like the arm movements of a "four count grapevine," and you could have some flexed wrists overhead or at your sides that all resemble the moves of the roaring 20s.

Shorty George

Can you imagine a country western dance complete with slapping thighs on beats two and four, rocking fists like a walking cowboy, the swinging of an imaginary lariat, or even the holding of the reins of an imaginary horse?

Country Western

How about floppy wrists in front at waist level, overhead, one up one down, low sway snaps, one hand on your waist with the other hand overhead pointing your index finger like a footless "Truckin" move for a great 1940s routine? Sugarfoot, jump back claps on two and four without actually doing the jumps, and even footless jitterbug routines are all possibilities for riser bound performers.

1940s moves

The dances of the 1960s or 70s can also be modified to work on the risers. Use The Monkey, The Jerk, Hand Jive, The Swim, The Search, The Watusi, and many others without ever having to move your feet! It really works!

SEQUENCES, RIPPLES AND WAVES

Notice how musical the "STADIUM WAVE" can be. Moves executed one person at a time, small or large groups at a time can be interesting to watch (and they use up a lot of counts!) Try clapping sequentially. Clap bursting, praying, saluting, nodding, changing of focus, bowing, standing up, sitting down, any move in slow or rapid sequence makes for great riser choreography!

HOW TO SIT ON RISERS

How many times have you wanted one section of your choir to "disappear" while you feature another section or a soloist for a song? Perhaps you have wanted to vary your programming with a "men only" number or a "women only" routine, yet you do not want to take the time to have the rest of the choir exit the staging area. It is not improper to have the non-singers sit right down on the risers and seemingly drop out of a number. They are however still participants in the selection if they are view of the audience. Actually, your "sitters" can do a lot to direct the focus and attention of the audience and create an interesting picture on stage.

It is important to instruct your performers as to how to sit on the risers. All should usually have their knees together and facing the performing person or group. If they are also looking at the performers, they will show the audience where to look. Notice how "unfriendly" it appears if the sitters do not have their attention directed to the performers.

Do not allow the performers to sit with their feet dangling off the side of the risers or stretched over several steps unless you are interested in presenting a very casual portrait.

Focus directed to center group

Focus directed to side group

AT EASE OR STAND BY

This is simply a stance that the performers assume to indicate that they are ready to begin. One possibility is similar to the "at ease" posture of a soldier, hands in the small of your back, feet either together or shoulder width apart, focus straight ahead. It displays a certain amount of discipline, helps adjust spacing between performers, and aids in focusing attention for the work to begin.

Stand by position

GRAB SEAM OF PANTS

Most hand problems occur because the performer has not been given specific enough direction as to what to physically do with them. Especially with younger performers, it is not inappropriate to have them actually hold the seam of their pant legs in order to develop the habit of keeping their hands at their sides. Or, specifically instruct them to extend their fingers down the sides of their leg, or make fists at their sides, or fistettes. Give them a definite assignment so that they will know exactly what you expect them to do. "Put your hands at your sides" may not be a specific enough direction for a fidgety fourth grader or nervous church choir tenor!

CONCLUSION

This little book is just the tip of the iceberg with regards to what a creative director can stage with his/her performers even when faced with very confined space limitations. It is an easily observed fact that young people of either gender like to wiggle. As I said before, in some ways a good choral director may just look at staging for entire choirs of young people as nothing more than "controlled wiggling." This is not a negative observation at all, but merely an undeniable rite of youth.

One of the many reasons that most directors of choirs do so is because they love the act of conducting itself, leading the choir through musical adventures with waving arms, nodding head and swaying torso. The bottom line is that it *feels* good. It is another facet of the musical experience we should wish upon all of our students and choristers. It seems, then, a selfish notion that the choir director who stands waving, nodding and swaying in front of his/her choir should expect them to stand rigidly, and quite unmusically, in place. Allow them to feel what you feel, express as you express!

The good news is that there is no limit to what you, the director; you, the musician; you, the artist can do when it comes to creating and staging your music. There are no absolute rules of which you should not experiment. No "right" or "wrong" in an art form that is forever dynamic. How wonderful to see the visual end of our musical world expanding in front of us with its boundless potential for creativity!

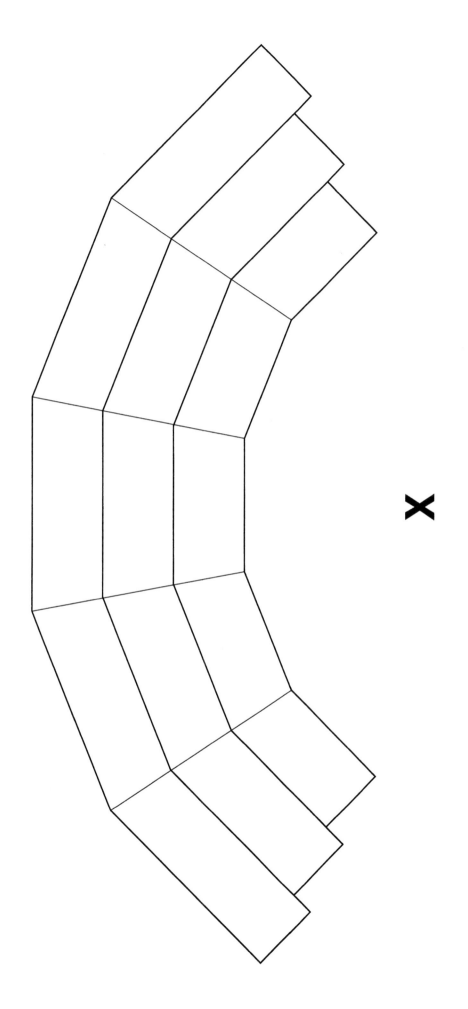

X